LONG PASS

JOEY CONNOLLY grew up in Yorkshire, studied in Manchester and now lives and writes in London. He co-founded *Kaffeeklatsch* poetry magazine, and has been the manager of the Poetry Book Fair for several years. In 2012 he received an Eric Gregory Award, and he has been Writing Fellow at the University of Manchester. His poetry featured in Carcanet's *New Poetries VI* (2015).

T0167934

JOEY CONNOLLY

LONG PASS

CARCANET

First published in Great Britain in 2017 by
Carcanet Press Limited
Alliance House, 30 Cross Street,
Manchester, M2 7AQ
www.carcanet.co.uk

A CIP catalogue record for this book is available from the British Library,
ISBN 978 1 784103 28 6

The publisher acknowledges financial assistance from Arts Council England.

Supported using public funding by
**ARTS COUNCIL
ENGLAND**

'Better the erratic approach, which wins all or at least loses nothing, than the cautious semifailure; better Don Quixote and his windmills than all the Sancho Panzas in the world...'

John Ashbery, *Three Poems*

FOR TERI, NIGEL AND JUDE

CONTENTS

1. Theories

2. Windmills

1. Theories

It's a poem about a father insulating his family home,
written some time in 1924. It notices, the poem,
the knotted rope of his spine through his
flannel workshirt as he hunches to the skirting;
his intent fingers working loose the dark wood,
panel by panel, and pressing in material from the roll of

asbestos matting behind him. With love he does the work
that fathers do. With aching thumbs he rocks the tacks
back into their beds, as the poem tucks its nouns into their gullies,
investing itself as fully as it can in how this father,
out of the dust of 1919, this father surrounds with love his
young wife, their new son. It drags and it dwells on this love,

it stalls and weeps for it, almost, this love inhabiting 1919
and written of in 1924. There's love in the way panels are pried up
and replaced. And something else. How the poem's author, reading
of the Medical Board's classification of asbestosis
in 1925, how she was reminded of that young wife arriving home,
and the pride already metastasising inside the husband how

she'd never know   how anything behind the boards had changed.

THE DRAFT

First this. Who is speaking? Careful,
it's dark. No, no, say *careful, the darkness
is brimming with something.* Yes.

First this: who is speaking? Careful,
the darkness is brimming with something.
With what? The darkness is swarming
with resolution. First this: who is

speaking? Careful, the darkness is swimming
with resolution. Put your hand out.

CHEKHOV'S GUN

From a train, she passes how all things pass, wrapped
in their instants, messy and simple as the as-yet unlooked-at

complication, under the sign for a rail-station named Marsden –
which is like the surname of a first love, from

before I understood, like now – standing alone,
the inscrutable woman, all cheekbones

and short hair, and red polkadots rapped onto their white,
her hand raised to rest against her cheek. *Life,*

for Chekhov, is neither horrible, nor happy,
but strange-unique-fleeting-beautiful-awful, according to Gerhardie

in this book I was reading before I shot by and saw the lee
of the sign for Marsden. *And for me, also* — and for me.

There but for the conciliatory haze of fiction go I.
There but for the crazy kindness of strangers
go our crises of conscience. There
but for the salt wind off the sea
goes the gold-drenched memory of 1992's
family holiday. There but for the graze of fog go we.

There but for the winnowing of Yahweh
go so many of our quaintest folk-statuettes. There
but for the faintest sense of justice
goes the conciliatory haze of fiction. There but for the
uncomfortable persistence of humanity
goes the neighbourhood.

There but for the harrowing frequency of laundry-days
goes the grace of god. There but for the slough of despond
goes our Christian. There but for one specific curtain of
palm-fronds goes the amber clarity of our faith.

There but for the goes of going walks our lord. There
but for the gauze of saying so goes all.

THE RIDER'S SONG

two versions of 'Canción de Jinete' by Federico García Lorca

I.

Córdoba. Apart
and apart.

Powder-dark horse; charged moon;
unpitted olives loose-panniered and khaki.
A road I believed familiar spells itself out
strangely, uninflected by memory
                          or Córdoba.

Through dust and across dust
(powder horse; flame moon)
there's a death
                 aware and waiting
in the wings and the spires
                     of Córdoba.

Ah so long road!
Ah powder-fine horse, stoic and disintegrating!
Ah patient death, that
        skilful interception. Córdoba!

Córdoba! Córdoba.
           Córdoba.

II.

Córdoba: romantic
and apart, and – the *Instituto Cervantes* research grant
blown on olives – lonely as this
bedsit study. I slant my pen to see

an ink-dark horse; an A5 of moon;
unpitted olives loose-panniered and khaki; and,
parting from the river, a road
I considered familiar spelling itself out strangely,
uninflected by memory – *Córdoba*. The word
       is unpocketable as the place.

Through dust and across dust, as
desert and air alternate furiously around
a blinkered horse, a tired-to-bloodshot moon. My eyes,
they weaken. I lose my hands to the sand-laden air,
my thoughts to the pull of *Córdoba*, and my pony,
its becoming its shape, its name. I cannot separate myself.

Ah! Road like a ten-clause-sentence!
Ah! Inky and well-meaning and disintegrating pony!
Ah, my glasses returning to sand, my cash
       to blank discs and paper, and I
all a word loses to its repetition. Córdoba.

  Córdoba.
        Córdoba.

FIRST LETTER FROM THE FRONTIER

'Mearc', Old English: mark, sign, character, boundary, limit

Our Bishop has stationed us at borders
and on boundaries, to force up a congregation – to find what passes
through these mountains as we can – and has gone into the night.

We plucky few with our taken orders
held out flower-like to these unlettered masses, an information
their crass tongue is proof against. Thus I write,

put down this mark which drives between us,
pressing me into the paper and you
outward from it, to breathe out in the piercing air

of the world, bounded by its skies of bone and water. Thus
I am alone. So much unnamed: the trees, their branches. What's true
rises from what's sweet like incense smoke. But here

every written word's a convoluted signature
and every painting seems a drawing of a picture.

[UNTITITLED]

for AW

The orthodontic meddling of language
with the world, its snaggling malocclusions
between a group of objects and their name

or the unnameable collusion of object and fact which
fritter truth like a spendthrift thrush
its energy in song. The determined unorthodoxy
in the solitary stance of a dock leaf, miles

from the nettles we suppose are its cause.
All I want is to tell you that I love you,
but how to trust that craft – its shoddy caulk – on those

bracing seas between us? And the jaws have
already sprung closed over the moment, albeit gappily.
And I am stung into refuge among such

exquisite cosmetic meaninglessnesses as the
awkward stagger of a branch across the sky above me as it
divides the blue into jagged, arbitrary portions.

All I want is to propose that we be wrong
in corresponding ways.

BEAUTIES OF THE NORTHWEST

I. *a daytrip to the Yorkshire Sculpture Park*

which comes back to you in drifts of memory
the shape of the sculptures,
the properly mysterious knotting and bunching
of Merlot-black materials, metals
and white marble and fibreglass, as if
the Yorkshire air had been ruffled
and calloused into solidity, or like scrap,
these jeep-sized bits of space, trailing their
explanatory plaques, weather-lacquered
and futile; trailing their talk of
bringing out the inherent resonance
of material; a mystery, a mystery to you; mysterious also
the meaning other visitors found or appeared to in these
dense clutterings of properties, these pieces of space that rest
so heavy on the haunches of their predicates.

But the lunchtime conversation
in the tea-shop was a good one, hard
to understand now, the ideas
catching between the teacups and the scones,
but clear is the feeling of something
being hammered out between you
and your parents, of a thought coming together
in the mouths of a youth counsellor, an antique restorer,
and a student. Something about
how beauty is best understood as a way of seeing,

so – the way a river is always busy with carving
the route it will come to flow, or the pose of a question
so often describes the shape

of its answer, or how a sound
cuts a noise-shaped gully
in your attention to settle into – the reach
of your looking, its rough branch, can be
stripped and whittled   to a molecule-fine point
of concentration. And between the scones and teacups
our words given shape
by the idea they fail to complete.

II.   *a walk around Manley Park*

which is heralded – out of the comfortable
white district you live in – by the boxy, uniform terraces
and a woman whose headscarf happens
to match the fading hydrangeas, leaning
over the garden walls, hovering
like a collection of hopes
over the pavement.

Around the corner small niqabis gather
around a burqa'd woman, making
birds of their hands, hooking thumbs and forcing
wings from the wave of their fingers; you cross the street

to avoid intruding, to offer
the olive branch of attention
to decorum. So it's this neat frame
of mind, walking home,
the woman steps into, with a movement
inside you – a wash
of ruffled blood – as much as of herself, her

body, appearing from its tiny
terraced house, old gold–shade sari-wrapped and so off-key
with her pebbledash surround, olive-and-marble eyes
only for her rotund goddamn husband
swinging his car door closed; she neuters
all other prettinesses
at a stroke. So you think of

how much beauty and detail
could be contained in every one of these
tidy domestic units, and you think
of atoms giving off their
minute particles, parcels of the most
immeasurable quantities of energy, barely keeping
it down, holding it together in their radiant
pink-gold glow, or electric-blue, and you walk

back past the globing hydrangeas,
a system of complicated hopes
floating over the August pavement.

SIX FILTERS

Every quitter carries in their greyer pockets a marginal awareness
of the number of filters they possess, and papers,
and of how much tobacco there is, and if the lighter
still burns at the first attempt: the mental dance
between these poles a waltz in the Aeolian mode.
And Ireland Argentinas as Egypt Burmas. Little Librans,

all of us; all of us scientific calculators upon which
precocious teenagers first discover the possibility of typing
obscene words. Your eyes blur as Rome burns, and it's the lack of
    focus
which matters most. We are stacked odds, and the means
to decidedly obscured ends. And the backs of all our minds
are the stats sections of long-discarded football cards,

and Greece Irelands as Syria Egypts, and the fingers
move across the keys they are able to reach.

FAILED STATE

I.

So for the time it takes to exhale
everything is breathing together, the quiet, the blood
in your glad-rags, in this battered
and sweet-smelling jeep, somewhere
on these new borders of former Rhodesia.
The air, set to echo. The glass sand.

II.

Everything goes heat-hazy
with what feels like
but isn't held breath.
When it goes, this stillness, it will go down
like a country collapsing, currency
skittering from control, the cop's revolver
in a blockbuster: the conceit
is excuse for a fistfight, for a brawl. Yes,

countries could collapse and people die
in droves and what's important
would be those moments
of intensest experience in the extinguished lives
of the deceased. Isn't it. Their rattling brevity, the failed states
of ecstasy. Yes, the senate falls and the priesthood

goes to ground, and the national bank
shuts its doors. The state falters
and goes down – once, for all – taking
its market partners with it and so

any hope of resurface. Bread disappears
from the market-stalls, women appear on doorsteps
waving their stubborn arms at reporters
from the first world. They begin to look like seaweed
swaying, unconscious and miles from the good
dry oxygen of the IMF. People return to custom

as they will in such times; headscarves
begin to reappear – the divorce rate plummets,
awfully. Children rehearse the national anthem,
and dictators mass on the sidelines. The place

is begging for a Junta as you shudder your last breath
into the handkerchief I hold – for no reason – to your lips.

Or not. There is a death: a moment,
a person, a country. What matter
which? States arrive, touching the sides
pleasurably as they do. Easy go, easy go.

CONTENT

You died in the back of a Cairo cab
thinking of a man wrapped in: bandages
and the twenty thousand tonnes of sandstone
it takes to point a pyramid at the sky.
Another time you died outside a Calais café
tasting a coral-pink macaroon in the February air.
On the drive to a Stockholm hotel you remember
dying on the steps of a university library,
a handsome dark-haired man bending to restore
your dropped books and each death was only
a part of that starry arsenal of memory from which
you had daily recrafted your idea of home
slipping off. The foundations
are not the thing, the contents
of the cupboards are not the thing, the draught
both entering and escaping is not
that thing. But there are bandages, there is indication
and there is cold air, and every carven moment
will shed the memories we have of it
like you, slipping from an old, comfortable bathrobe
into a death of body temperature and steam.

COMING TO PASS

two versions of a fragment ('Reif Sind, in Feuer getaucht, gekochet...') by
Friedrich Hölderlin

I.

The way fruit, arriving
at its moment of ripeness, is glazed with fire,
cooked and checked by the earth's close process. It's law,
after all, how all things
come to pass, temptress
but unearthly. And as
the heavy stake of kindling, resting
on the shoulders, there is much to bear
in mind. But the trails
are evil. And everything
bridled will anyhow
wander off, like horses
into dusk; everything
shot-through with this longing
to go beyond bounds. But so much
stands to be lost. And loyalty
a must; which rules out prophecy
or nostalgia. Let us surrender, be rocked –
cradling ourselves against the moment –
like a boat, lapped by the waves.

II.

For a moment the project
will come perfectly to fruition,
each word glossed by its
plunge into the fire of the present, that flicker

from which everything is once again
made anew. It's almost gospel
the way things arrive, slip askew,
and depart: as a snake,
dreaming of the cloths of heaven, its mounds
of laundry, its drying lines. And as
the weighted intellect is kindle
to any moment's inspiration
or distraction, there is much to bear
in mind. And the previous versions
of the damn thing verge
on the diabolical. And everything
you think you've got bridled, every axiom
you've nailed, will wander off, like horses
into dusk, appearing
to dissolve into the dust of secondary
and tertiary meanings. And the constant
temptation to reach beyond what's
suitable, beyond bounds, into the dense red
of yourself, your vague
and useless gloss. And so much,
so much stands to be lost! And loyalty
a must: this raking up of foreign soil –
the spoiled quarantine of adherence
to original – is no good. No good. All of which
rules out the possibility of prophecy,
or nostalgia. Let us rock between the two,
like a little skin-keeled coracle on a sea of confusion,
lapped by the various camberings
of serial and distinct waves, one
after the other, made up
of the exact same water.

NETHERLANDS

Ann's Story

I was any three-year-old: a dream of curiosity. If you see
an open door you go through:
that's what doors *are*. An inconstancy

of right and wrong – of action and its kinds of truth
had inhabited my vacation head
that holiday – the Netherlands, Nineteen-fifty-two.

And the bright suburban street's nearest door was ajar, and my tread
still absence-soft enough to pass whichever off-guard parent,
and I was in.   I remember a bed,

and solider even than its dark-wood frame the astonishment
at the eyes – on me! – of the woman half-amid the sheets,
small and dense: a surprise of curves. I've spent

such heavy hours since, retreading these curving streets
of the words I've hung on every memory I've had
of those wavering Netherlands, wholly incomplete

by now with passing through and through of that Dutch red,
half-hoping still to find a heart of flesh among the deep white
of empty sheets; and every memory a now-vacated, still-warm bed.

and for all there is no other thing
in which the soul or any soul-like thing consists:
clear as lipstick is lips. Or the free will
of one hand, moving for another: a vanity. A sun,
spun around the Earths we weave of ourselves.

I do not say this. I watch you watching the moon.
And any moment I will take my chest and I will kiss you.
For the first time. And so to the materialist I say:
if you can't ride two horses at once
you shouldn't be in the circus.

AN OCEAN,

two versions of a fragment ('Antico, sono ubriacato dalla voce...')
from 'Mediterraneo' by Eugenio Montale

I.

antiquer by far than the best furniture my father
was given to restore, to piece together from other woods,
to fix, and I'm hammered with the voice
that hauls itself from all your mouths, opening
into the moodswing gape of bells, greenish
and self-effacing, ringing into nothingness
and returning. I lived here once, at your shore, the sun
making a midday bakery of every point between these
three horizons, mosquitoes thickening the air. And so I

thicken back into presence, only now
lacking the target-part for the dressing-down
you have for me, the short shrift under your
breath. You showed me
how the petty unrest of my heart
was just a moment's symptom of yours,
your cause; that down at the seafloor of my

life is that incomprehensible absolute:
to be the occurring shift of hugeness, its change and still
to be fixed in place. And so to slough off, like you
the rubble and filth of myself,
the dregs and starfish of your abyss.

II.

and 'ocean' is as good a term as any
for the startless thing

you are, and anyhow I'm stripped
of agency, reckless drunk
with a voice which springs from all your mouths –
the bells and pretty lines, the confessions and recollections I can't
keep from getting in,
from soaking what good people have made dry.
I try to find a way the voices
can rise and dissolve into the stuff
they're of. Like waves, but ideas have words
and words ideas and they get
everywhere, sand in sandwiches
at the beach. I think, helplessly, of the place
I used to live; I *Sheffield* and I thicken.
I make recollections like new bread and I absentee myself
from the proper rigours of responsibility. You showed me
the shallows of my heart, how its storming
was only a fractal part of the language
in which it stormed: that down at the seafloor of my life
is that   incomprehensible absolute: to be

III.

what Morgan calls *as various as vast,*
yet fixed in place, – the stability I imagine
of constant renewal, of permanent momentum; the gyroscope
steadied by the movement
of its elements. Galassi
has *voracious* for *vast,* and *fast*
for *various.* And so to work, so
to slough off, like you, the rubble and filth
of myself, the seaweed and the starfish of your abyss.

SOME PECUNIARY OBSERVATIONS

Like a hopelessly bourgeois but charming market town
in the heartlands, in which
the moment the poetry festival ends
the In Bloom horticultural extravaganza
grows inaugurate. Town criers in regal blues
roam the squares, ringing bells,

the pealings of which startle upwards
like the sudden flight of noisome, heraldic birds.
Oh heartlands, you garlanded warehouse
of cherished ideals and cosy ropes of conjecture;
you trader motoring to the market town
with a trunkful of chintz you know you'll shift

at magnificently bemargined prices. Accordingly
and moreover, the pursed lips of the very beautiful;
the conclusive redundancy of simple pleasures
in the face of those yet simpler. The barter
of comfort for hope. Oh heartlands,
you total 24/7 engine of destruction.

I'm getting surer
it's inescapable,   this
way of doing things   the leaves   on trees   have,
the dull madness   of profusion,   the tumble
of identicals,   the huddle

of uniformed kids   breaking out
      into a wild   but contained game
of chase or   tag or kiss-chase   at the slightest tug
            of a breeze

so this   insane design,   this   drunken Fibonacci –
      as fast   as we replace it
   with brick   and facility   it reasserts itself
      – the tumble,   the frantic   contact –

   in the play of meaning   over meaning,
so our   signs – perfectly   dichromatic
      oblong boards   reading *Pandora's*   or
                Sam's Auto Parts   –   start, at the first

      drift   of the mind,   leafing
through the banks of their   noirish associations,   their
   bluey steam   of suggestion,   and so
we're back   at that   familiar   same-thing-again-

   and-again   that leaves have   of running
         against each other   and together,   of being
identical looking, only   not quite,   (it being
                no coincidence,   the way

the spinal rippling   of a river   close-up
            sets itself   so firmly   against the sill
of its shore,   the way
     the shiver of leaves   is only   a shiver
                against one   or other   implacable   sky)

        which is

        your mind   repeating the functions
     which just take   nature's shape,   its bundle
of angles,   and the green
        and the green   of unstopping

CARRYING

The pigeons carry their reputation for disease like a canker
hidden in the beak. They peck mechanically about my feet
in my Thames-side café: the bitterer the coffee the more here I feel
in the same drowse of survival they bespeak, filthy doven clods

of proof for evolution. They carry their reputation for disease
like a sixties schoolgirl her clothbound volume of Sartre,
mildewed and risky. The pigeons are iron furbelows
ruffling the café patio's concrete flagging. How much really do I need

to confront myself with history? I could raise my eyes
to the thin, pigeon-crowded piers like dark tongues
furred with nerves for the determined endless tasting of the old
river. Lucy and I held hands again for the first time last night

since the final kiss of our long relationship; my father had tickets
to the game that became the Hillsborough Disaster.
My mum's father stole his older brother's passport
to escape Ireland for the Second World War. But that's

all over now, truly; and my dad was called, last-minute,
to work. And my grandfather returned, though not again
to old Ireland; ferried that inaccurate, harped passport
to Dagenham, where at last he made my mother. Essex girls

have such a reputation and are surely proof
that none of this has any value whatsoever. Think of her –
outside the secondary modern in the shadow of Ford's
relentless heavy plant – a new flagship of French existentialism.

It's only that each thing carries another. The tongue,
so evolved, has five types of cell for tasting: my own
is deficient at savour and has nothing at all for the forces
which have brought over time these things to their being.

A man is falling asleep in the plush comfort
of a hotel armchair, a lit cigarette trembling
barely between his fingers. Any moment the air will grow
hot to the touch with the discomfort of inaction. Later
the windowframes will take, the light-fittings themselves
drift in imperceptible degrees from a plastic white
to the vaguely patterned brown of inattention, the plush armchair
to fire in a room of fire.

Elsewhere a painter is at his concentration.
He measures out his attention like a liqueur,
ignoring the mild furore of the late sun, its fading glare
seeming to ruffle the sea it lights on. A sea, as usual,
he can barely ignore. His still life
both stills and saturates its oranges;
the sharp edges of the table fray
and give as they approach the costly blue
of the vase; the fruit bowl
ceases to contain that fruit
which falls below its lip and out of the hard line of sight.

The gaze abstracts as it objectifies; object
bleeds into type, the starvation-ration of quiddity,
the hardtack of category, like interlocking
fingers – the posture of an infinitely sympathetic refusal
cast off
across the copper-inlaid oak of a café coffee table,
perhaps in a piazza of Venice, maybe
years ago now, before that thennish city
was understood to be sinking – the gesture
descending to a scrimshaw, sunk into still-living bones.

In every Western ever made
there's a cowboy, his face a cave of oranges
and greys in the campfire's, yes, flickering light.
He's an exacting mechanistic archetype of machismo, sure,
but is pictured as somehow one with nature, running his
calloused hand across the rope-burned collar of hide
decorating the neck of the lassoed steer, damaged
by the way we gather it to us.

In the evolving technology of chess piece manufacture the
unrefined chits of maple and rosewood are known as *blanks*.
We remove from them what's unnecessary until the desired
form is attained. The desired form is one that signifies only
within the system of rules of the game for which it's intended.
Remove a bow of wood here and here and the piece will move
maybe three spaces instead of four. Pieces meant for finer sets
receive their inlay. After, one of two varnishes will be applied.

Adjectives queue like interior designers
fingering the fabric samples for the refitting
of a burnt-out hotel room. The felt swatches of material claim their
     titles
only insofar as they defer to another scene, absent
and imagined. Like the flamboyant designers they specify
at the same time they subject themselves
to something larger. We have such a mania for outfitting.

Reach out; alter into an admittable shape; utilise.
Place the grey scent of an old twenty pence piece
into the slot below a seaside telescope. Turn to your mother

The chemical the human brain employs
in the access of a memory
          (the fingers of a perfume

and a person and an ideal
description of a perfume interlocking
imperfectly, that
vase)
is also the chemical that reaches in to rearrange
the synaptic pattern – the stick mandala
of an unlit campfire – which
incarnates that memory; that
which once again unchars these sticks anew.
As new, still-wet permanent marker is the best plan
for erasing old permanent marker, being in a place
is the best way to undo that place. Try
as best you can
to hold on to what it is we face
now – that charlatan, that impostor.

It's an artist's impression of the world, a reconstruction
of the chase, after the fact,
the unsentenced con mid-getaway, face turned
briefly to camera, Remington '58
full-chambered with blanks. Steer. Hide.
                                    The uniform surface of the sea
speaks of the gross magnitude of a suffocating
nothingy fullness settled over by its surface.
Your child's handful of gaze skates out across its plain
its low waves and points of light in the late sun
unprocessable tonnage of data
happily encompassed in this moment of you, your attention
agitating butterfly-like at the horizon. Twelve years
you'll meet someone called

The painter is frustrated to be always
painting *onto* something, to be
concealing precisely as he displays.

The odour of the tincture he requires
to mix the precise tone of cerulean
tastes the air with the tongue of an old lover; so
the body of his work is just overwhelmingly seascape.

'What are we as a species if not a carving out from
the wooded, wet earth we evolved in reciprocal
counterfactual to? I am the sum of a string of a white
man's failed relationships. I am a messy desk and a stack
of unread books, the constant dull subpoena of alcohol
and tobacco.' See the way the tone veers uncontrollably?
and I reach for the lead of type, the steadying semicolons
and pilcrow and the scattering of inverted commas.
And I reach to steady myself against the balustrade of a
formulated phrase, and I tally the scars on her forearm,
and I count the days, closing like a five-barred gate.

and Rome burning
becomes the world. But no,
focus. Greece,
Greeks: '...this
incoming fire meets a fire moving
towards it, and the outgoing fire
leaps out like lightning
while the incoming is quenched
in moisture', which is Plato,
flicking his basically unconvertible
fifty cents into the
frankly unnatural
science of human sight,
that wishing well,
that reservoir – the seascape
they're inseperable from.
Every state

steady enough
to be expressed
is the result of a negotiation between chaos
and chaos. But so
since Plato it's sight has been
the burning rope bridge
by which we approach the world
firstly, and not
taste, or hearing, because the world is mostly
human faces, the flickering of the
sad, uncertain smile onto and from your
Greek lips, delivering

'But in what measure the quantities should be mixed,
it would not be wise to say, even if one knew.'

See how the tone veers uncontrollably under the pressure
of what presses up from everything uncaptured by the
implicit network of rules, the script, the proscriptions
of grammar. The bowl struggling to contain its oranges;
the signature its mark of presence; the painting its
subject; the cards their interpretation; the icecaps
their carbon; the translator his reading; the gendered
body its outrageous fusillade of demand and counter;
the mother her child and child her mother; the poem
its egotism of ambition; the painting its subject;
the skirting its malevolent clad. The hotel room its
design, its unconscious inhabitant. The hide its steer;
the cowboy his flowering weakness; the last letter
from the frontier its creepy desire; the past its lovers;
the explicatory framework its political positions and
general gross mass of presupposition; the gullies their
forest of nouns; the race the thriving narrative of race;
the memory its content; the game its rioting players; the

world its ruthless inhabitants; the currency its inflation;
the scrimshaw its skeleton; the skin its skeleton of
ideology; the gesture its whole personal history

The gutsy tango of information through
this thick triple sec–and–candyfloss broth,
the fibreoptic bordello of undercooked pork-knuckle
and skittering haptics, of dancing girls
in paroxysms of echoic memory,
the dopamine-stoked homunculur designer
ransacking his cowboyish saddlebags of
sovereign instants for the face of a first love
who is no, not the same, changed
by the light of even a moment's exposure.

Steer. Hide. To be
at-one-with implies
being reached into,
too. Cowboy. Fool. And until then

the silver-grey fifty-cent piece and your mother
and notice only now the blue of her eyes,

And what could be plusher than experience? The intense
cornicing and fretwork of imagination and memory
inlaid in everything like veins, like the pipes
of a sprinkler system in a paper mill. Description
· is the finest fire-proofing we have,
an insulation from the inhumanity
of the too real. It is the cell wall we tap on,
with the zinc frame of our pince-nez, our faint signals
to the intriguing criminal next door – the world as is,
that thief, that fraudster, that arsonist.

THE BIG HOUSE

Amateur musicians start up unexpectedly so
a kind of music I know nothing about –
baroque or symphonic, or chamber – plays,
in slow notes, flat with the smell of instant coffee,
and dry toast, and unmarked hardback books, across this

hangover of mine, couched in its now-useless hideout, which
overlooks the grand-house's grounds, across which flit
unknown birds, thrushes maybe – blue-tits, swallows –
like a display of emotion I shouldn't think
I could put a name to it's so joyful.

HISTORY

A version of 'History' by Robert Rozhdestvensky

History! / Picture me, a young man, so / naïve, so deeply
believing / and sincere / over your
absolutes, your palette / of trues. Your / precision of gradient
and angle, / indisputable as a math; / less questionable
than cliché. / But boys / age, become
grown. Your wind / shades their skin / and the seconds now
are demanding account / of the centuries. / I write
in the name / of the seconds...

History / has the fructose / beauty of
dawn. History / has the grand / grind of poverty,
structuring people anew / before / scuttling off
in the face of their / degradation. History / correct
and senseless. Recall, / now, how frequently / you're called
appalling, though / breathtaking, or / *noble* though shocking,
shameful, / cruel. / How you depended
on passing / fashion, on ego / and conception:
on dumb façade. How you / shrunk / from the dictators
who measured you / by their own / invented versts and the scrabble
of inches. / Proclaiming your / name, they
stupefied the peoples, / claimed / your protection, and made
worlds / lands. You have allowed yourself / to be
powdered, / history, again: rouged and / made up,
again, and redyed, / and again fitted / for a suit of new black.
You were / redrafted / to that
army / of / raucous cries
specialising / in switching 'great men' / for people:

History! Whore. / *History!* Queen. / You are not
the dust, drying / in archives. History, / clutch these whispering
    fingers,

open your / living heart / to the people.
Look, / how / sensibly
your founders, / your / managers and copers
are waking, / are / swallowing their
humble breakfast. / They are hurrying / to kiss their wives,
their goodbyes. The greenery / of scent covers them, so / excitingly,
    the high
sun / beats in their eyes, / the horns
flourish their / noise, / and the imperturbable smoke
rises endlessly / from the chimneys; / cries its tired praise against
the still sweep / of skies. / You will,
history, / you will be yet / the most exact
gauge and measure, / the sweet geometry / of pressure. You
will be. You must. / It is so / longed-for.

2. Windmills

These days I order my coffee black, like an actress
making it. I take a seat, feeling either landlocked
like a thinking-man's seagull or like a B52 held painfully
in reserve. And the concrete-locked sailboats outside

say *Topaz Sailing System* on them, and the people
boating on the reservoir all say *Swarovski Coping System*
in them. The water fails in the February grey to glisten,
but the whitenesses of loosed gullfeather can act up,

stand in. Like I understudy the reservoir,
heft my participation mystique like a medicine ball between
my stomach and the low wishbones of my cheeks.
I check my phone continually, like an agent.

The lake and my indoorsman idea of the lake go at it
like boxers, hell-for-leather, like-for-like, then seem briefly
to embrace, like boxers often will. The reservoir
is like a lake. The café an elsewhere. I check my phone,

and head outside to join the Portuguese man ostensibly
manning the till – now disking bread disconsolately to the seagulls –
and to listen to the wind and the construction-work, the wind
and the seagulls, and the asthmatic crackle

of a cigarette with too-little tobacco at its filter end.
And to gaze like an actress across the wind
and the reservoir's shocked terrain. And Chris Isaak
whispers 'Wicked Game' to the deserted café behind me *It's strange*

In those days, the brusque burlesque of certain barriers
between us and the world
of others dissolving
in the viscous base solution of chance.
The clicky physics of a parabola
in high-impact plastic
entrance-permissioned for the depthiest passages of that
needful hopey den you pass through and into,
recursively. Those days
of all self-contained matter smug in its primacy
over the web of certainties you carry. In those days
all tenets of epistemology shot, a small man
held up against a plasterboard wall,
his inherited tailored waistcoat
coming open at the seams, becoming
not a waistcoat. In those days, becoming rags.
In those days, as in the roughhouse of expression, trusting yourself
to the warm hands of chance and suggestion.
In those days as in war a sudden starkness
of the bonds held within opposition, the threads binding pawn
    and peon
alike. I'm sorry. In those days the colourful percussive language
of men staring their own weakness
in the eyes, and with all the rich rags of our century's manliness
staring it down. The insignificance
of their disappointment. In those B.O.D.S
a destitution hard to find
elsewhere. Find a level: chance and cash
are the same thing   remember. In those days,
the monolithic impersonality of the House,
glistering and rebarbative,
fraying at its industrial edges like an empire,

drowning in its own convoluted bureaucracy.
In those days the concussive exponential manufacture of hope.
The berlinesque coming down of walls,
the flood of one thing into another. Hope,
cash, the steady percussion of loss   paper. So much paper.
Those days an amphigory of loss, a clunky YA parable of
forfeiture, unfurled across the thousand instalments
of scrawled-on A6 betting-slips. An aspirational language
coating the nasty little facts like a sugar.
Remember this. The higher the register
the more to hide, the drawn
staked rhetoric of desperation. Days held in structure
by flashes of your own   unbearable face.
In the inch-thick Perspex   of the bandit shield.
That is   you look unbearably yourself. So that
something like   a history intrudes, narrative and sinewed,
accreting like a debt around a single, unpayable bill,
a cloud around its particles of dirt.
The tacky eschewal of ignorance. The becoming rags
of past caring. Those days. In the disappointment
of their insignificance. A small man, held up

COMPREHENSION TEST

Complete the sentence

How blank longs for greater blank

Try to bear in mind it's never

a case of changing one thing for another

WHAT YOU'VE DONE

i.m. Rachel Jardine

or one thing you've done: thrown yourself
more hugely amongst
my neat web of signification, so that
ballet comes with a picture of you tacked to it,
so that *Sartre* has your scar by its
right eyebrow, and *jumper* your crazy smile,
and *blue* your birdlike nerves, your neatness,
the neat math of your thoughts, your thoughts.

And *bloom*, after the car-park of Bloom St., puts you
somewhere before Joyce's Bloom, but after –
even still – after a picture of an unnamed orange flower
from a textbook, under the German for *flower*. There's really
no connection   the net of implication
like everything comes apart in your hands.

of putting paid to the alarming rumours threatening their concept
    of self and reputation
of enacting the dumb charade of their own explanation
of unseating the tsar who's refusing their appeal for self-definition
of checking the bizarre ludic explosion of their own plausible
    interpretations at the hands
of the anarchic cackling deconstructionists
of piecing together the shards of last night's string of massive
    revelations
of tuning the guitar on which their anthem will imminently be
    composed
of bribing the guards to their own typically unmanned control-room
of turning the dive-bar's increasingly drunken chatter into
    uninhibited self-confession
of guessing the value of the coins in the cookie-jar of their budget
    for party political broadcast
of programming the VCR to record the pivotal climax
of what they're told will be, by far, their next favourite box-set
of unlearning the disarming modesty which so trivialises their
    social personae
of bribing sufficiently the bards who already are busy recording
    their legend
of going the whole-nine-yards to a true Buddhistic-style
    self-realisation
of chairing the seminar tasked with the slow process of their own
    exegesis
of hacking up conclusively the catarrh from the windpipe through
    which they will sing themselves
of definitively influencing the pronunciation of their own name
    c.f. Burma
of waving au-revoir to the charming if unoriginal beau of
just saying so   of insisting   of telling all of us just what in fact
    you are.

IN THE PROCESS

The microscopes began proffering all their mad doxological detail
in desperate excess of anything our species was ever likely to survive
long enough to see. It was then all these billionfold trivialities
    erupted,
immigrated woozily in to our formerly quiet, tidy lands,
all stamping tinily and wildly proclaiming
the randomness of the deal. It's the blackjack hand
of your mind laid against the cruel pontoon of the world,
all twos and fours but the point
is that it *feels* as if there were rules,
incapable though the cards are
of specifying the guide for their own interpretation.

Ach! I misspoke. What I mean to say is this:
there's a timeless fairground to-and-fro
between the reduced and therefore
manageable thing and the sprawling unmappable
backstreets of the actual,

that's all. In every Western ever seen
the spittoon by the beauty-queen bar-girls
is half-full with what has been
chewed over and jettisoned, obscene and therefore
fascinating. And never a hand of poker played fair.

And although that was then, still the rule-card for bridge
should properly never be shuffled into the pack before dealing:
that's the trick and the travesty both. It's our fractional moments
of access to the appropriate software for editing
those rule-cards which make all future rounds
of the tournament so chaotic and also
hilarious: the odds-on favourite,

a former philosopher in a looming nimbus of a hairdo,
clapping a well-read palm to his temple in outrage,
dislodging his prescription spectacles in the process.

THAT ROGUE LONGING

when it's otherwise all in order –
all settle and glister – every feeling
accounted for, all told: it occurs

like a gnat which skips my swat –
chip of will – squat loaf
of matter – bold little exister.

YOUR ROOM AT MIDNIGHT WAS SUDDENLY

Two versions of 'Ἀπολείπειν ὁ Θεός Ἀντώνιον' by C. P. Cavafy

I.

rich with the feeling of your hearing
an unseen procession, a procession rich itself
with the strains of its beauty, a low
darkness of voices – but now
                    is no time to mourn your loss,
your departing fortune – a life's work
spoiling before your eyes, a host of plans
proving illusory. As if you were
prepared, ever (as if you were brave),
say farewell to the Alexandria that is leaving.

And further: do not allow yourself
the lie of having dreamt, that your ears fail,
or your draining mind. Do not sully this
moment's song with the baseness of your desire
for stability. But as if

you were prepared, ever –
as if you were brave – move,
steady, to the window, as one
given for a city such as this,
this hugeness, move to the window and
beat with the pulse of feeling,
a feeling far off

from the pitched reed and entreaty of cowardice: no,
listen as a fatal delicacy to that voice,
that mass of beauty, that strange
and passing procession off

in the distant absence
of the Alexandria you are anyway losing.

II.

on the table because god knows I'm no
romantic but I
                want you. And underneath that
we sip our coffee and your eyes
are darker than any history or coffee, than any
Greek coffee ever was and hold the gloss
of depth only such darkness has. God knows
I want you to the point
of shucking the woman I love,
our house, the home we built
so slowly. And there is a procession offstage
which accompanies the upward swing
of your eyes, harmonises the argument
for discord, and you're explaining in an
almost unbroken English a poem from the Greek
of Cavafy: I don't know it. As if I were a coward

I keep quiet. On the table of my mind, I mean –
your room – hopeless
coward as I never thought
I was, hopeless neighbour of these
strains of romance language (the names
for your description, the country
my instinct will use to define you), close as I get
to the classicism of your Greek heart,
the close, Doric order of your form.
I don't know what it is which is leaving,
only the sweet draw of its
pain as it goes from me.

SATURATION

In the sun in Madrid there was something
about the shine of her hair and also if that complex
delicate net of self-worth has left her
less able to locate the proper value in others. From music school

in Berlin my brother complains of these days
hearing always music's patterned fade into production
and soundwaves, compression and lowpass filters
and saturation. The same way London's incredible

pooled blaze of communal brightness
has cost us our constellations. Or how it's possible,
in an eerie Toronto that still insists
seriously on Hallowe'en, to miss the actual ghoul

amid the clever, home-made costumes.
                                        That fucking hair.
How in the attempt to justify my disgusted pride
the search for the apposite putdown is like dodgems,
garish and glaring off their 1920's Illinois production line.

LOSS

What is it – reassurance? – I get
from the thought of obscure & complicated
numerical transactions occurring
in sad, former-Soviet towns,
in cold, dusty, Eastern-European townsteads ringed
by collapsing fences, in post-offices or
private rooms, with balance books
& iron-looking machines with
sliding parts & till-rolls or ribbons
& outdated conversion tables
to rely on, unlaminated & hopeless?

& when that post-Soviet economy went down
so much became worthless; but to know
that tiny, tangle-fine flares
of complication are going up, everywhere
and always: data is the only mark we can make
in the streaming tickertape of passing time.
But how to compare such
wonderful detail to the billions
that were lost in transaction, in conversion
to untranslatably richer currencies? How the light

settles in its million angles
on the leaves of the raspberry canes
which provide the primary export,
those sweet bright globes
which flow across borders, like fact
or rumour, handed from one person
to another, bound in their
rich units of red, rich

as the unthinkable desiderata
of bickering gods. And with what

loss, what adjustment
for conversion? Think of us, our words
& figures, the richness
of the detail we imply, our rituals
& calculations & lookings-up. How everything
is being set down, somehow, and nothing
at all is slipping past too easily.

If not spires then phone masts; not explosives
then the nagging ethics of democracy.
If not fresh paint then the toadskin upholstery
of the railings and ironwork
of this city's eastern reaches. If not now, well, then whatall
of the children we can make. If not
two nil then four three. If not hope
then parades; not bells then whistles.
If not the delicate tentacles of the ability
to cope then the wealth of the loam.
If not the epitome then the persuasive
stranger. If not the hiss and clatter of Autechre
or Venetian Snares through your old laptop's speakers
then a punitive silence: if not time
then service. If not a sparkling metropolis
then an arctic of peace, if not a riot
then an act. Try to remember
that in mixing any two of Ireland's finest wines
their exquisite and respective bouquets
will still engender piss. Remember this, and move always
as if to accept the lesser of the two. If not a blessing then a
genuine well-wishing; if not a lesson then a lyric.

ON LATTERLY OVERCOMING LAST OCTOBER'S LOSS

for Rosa Tomalin

Laugh out loud, oh lover of levity, our lingering optimism lightens our load. Observe, lover, our lashings of luxurious ornament: lilac oil, Lebanese ocarinas, legumes, oriental lanterns, oranges, lemons or limes; O listful of lissom, obdurate, lifely objects, lighting opulently like old-fashioned lamp-posts onto liveries of limbic obsidian; like object layered onto looser object. Listen:

our love of life ornaments life.

Oh! Lots of love! Outrageous levies on last October's loss! Outspoken lauding of linguistic observation! Lavish objections looming over lazy ontologies! Let others languish over lost opportunities: let's overturn long outstanding limitations. Our lovely organic laudanum obliterates longings, or lessens our lisping objections, or leastwise outlaws languor. Oh listing Occident, lapse outwards.

Lux. Omnia. Laeto.

THEMSELVES

I have learned the words – curlicue,
arabesque, craquelure – and I have done my best
to feel that well-spoken weft &c. beneath

the skin of things, with ketamines or caffeines
mingling with the bloodstream I have long
been shifting, twice changing between Liverpool Street,

between St Pancras and here. All preparation
dissolves like cardboard-minded
hangover-morning vitamin supplement at this

sudden coast, the mist-hung edges of this shingle beach,
its pitchless singing, its pebble-rattle intensifying
to the static hiss of unthinkable numbers, this

vast variegate of stone being
dragged across itself by the persistent
knowing drugged retreat

of the waves, and the gentle waves – patina, spindrift,
astringent – and the waves. The vast multiplication table
of its rattle. The mingling of the symbols for stones

with the symbol for seawater rinsing the two,
the three-inch give of a tortoiseshell of shingle
underfoot, the way every rounded collateral pressure

of stone on deeper stone comes up
through the shoesoles, the soles of the feet,
up through some rail-cartographer's dream of nerves,

up to the neck and the graze there of the salt-air
on the tongue, scouring off the need for words
and, a breath after that, the words

2018, 2017, 2016, 2015, 2014,

at an indeterminate point of a night
hot as an hourglass of finest Sahara familiar hands
remake the disorient echoing
chamber of your room and all of you

out of glass planes drawn implacably
across faces of schist and brass discs
so tenderly they will never break. Your world must
sometimes be the world. Rises again. Were it

some balaclava of the psyche... but it's not:
it's gas and rent and rail and all those
hyperreal almighty sappers which will
not be salved by any

shrink or deep breath or mythy tincture,
nor any counting backwards

DIDN'T JOKES USED TO BE FUNNY?

after Louis MacNeice

Time was away, and somewhere else. Pied birds
hung like muted baubles in the trees,
the leaves of which were proof against the
Christmas breeze of that shocking December day's

hour's minute's second. The word you will now
have forever chosen resting like an ice-cube
at half-melt on your red lower lip and I wondered slowly
where time had gone: off and elsewhere. Everything

suddenly had far too much detail; the stuff was pasted
crazily on, like glitter on a schoolkid's Christmas project.
Christmas had come so early it passed
unnoticed, and the Christmas after

loomed like a punchline, and then you're thinking
irrelevantly of shame, of what
a colossal fucking shame and that time was away
and somewhere unrecognisably else

had come rushing in to fill its place.

LIGURIA

On the one hand, there is the morning sunlight
insinuating itself helically with the fibres
of the canes and their dusty-leaved tomato plants

about them. On the other, the plump primary note
of a woodpigeon swelling rhythmically into the air
like the drop at the lip of a non-off tap, swelling

into the dialetheic air, clean but ripe, gamey, with its two
quick stabilisers: the *glue* goes. We *pool* so, it
schools us. The *rules*: yes, they fooled you, accruing...

The air is in the constant moment
of being rinsed so clean by the sunlight
that it vitrifies into sunlight, thin and brazen. And then

because light and air are ten things
it's thickened again by the baking masonry which insists
on a history magnificently, manifestly distinct

from the ferrous bramble it seems in England; a history
of certain people completing dignified tasks
in sonorous metals; of Indian summers both cruel

and unusual. But this brittle bauble, this Mexican standoff
of air, and light, and time avers   (re*too*ling)
what nonsense it is to talk   (it's *true*, Joe)

of elements. We are pylons of yew, made up
of the smell of dry grass, the scent of its silent rustle,
its quiver like a decision going unmade,

the glucose unspooling, the bluest undoing.

you are saturated with body, and inhabit it the way darkness
    disperses through water:
with shadows of deeper concentrate, wrecks yawing on the seabed
    with stowaways
of the least-known and so intensest hollows of attention, and
    potentially bright fish pushing
blindly at rusted bulwarks, miles from the surface we want to claim
    to like
best. You might be right that our obsession with the ends of things
derives from our thinking so much about sex,

or when we were young our thinking so much about sex. Younger,
    anyway:
remember the bluey darkness it used to be like
suddenly finding yourself in? Remember the obsession of sex with sex?
But your skin grows depearlescent, and the wrecks of old ideas
    become manifest as things:
they are the scurf of refuse on the surface of our old park's only pond,
    pushing
harmlessly at its borders. For only the hollow are awarded borders;
    think of water

with its no inner edge; the hollows it rushes to fill, like
it's been thinking only of erasing emptiness (because yes, this is
    amongst the things
staining the surface of our any tipsy talk of sex). Later, a tall cool
    glass of water
stands stilly in the darkness of a midnight kitchen, with midnight
    pushing
at the windows from the wrecks left of summer's only oak-trees,
    while nobody upstairs has sex.

If it is not to be a stain, then it must be an obsession. And if there is
	any way

of ennobling an obsession, it lies with the things
which obsess you being never left to ring hollow; in pushing
deeper into the wrecks of ideals made by the examples and
	instances which are anyway
all we have. It is the so-much thinking through which drags down sex
from its admittedly synthetic pedestal, which vexes the capacity of its
	darkness and waters-down
the intensity of the dissolution of your sole surface, the like-for-like

exchange of one surface giving onto another. Think of two men,
	breathlessly pushing
their broke-down Skoda home in the obsession they foster like so
	many of their sex
with self-reliance. Around them, darkness starts to fall, like
one hollow is growing inside a finer hollow, the water
from the cracked radiator thinking its thought-bubbles onto the
	tarmac, and anyway
the wrecked driveshaft as which these two men exist, now – far more
	than the things

and ways of their separate bodies – this wreck, jointly hauled, is as
	much sex
as anything is. Such facts are beginning to surface in our species, felt
	in the rough waters
surrounding the isle of our lord, that bent and thin king, reason.
	There are always things
swimming inwards with the press of obsession to find any way
of entering that hollow. And it will never be the mirror itself which is
	your lookalike.
Because it's the speculation as to what it is makes up our darkness
	which is pushing

this obsession with thinking things – like sex, like water, like darkness. It all makes wrecks of all these sensuous surfaces pushing outwards from the dark echoic hollows which is anyway all we are.

THIRD BALLAD

Two versions of 'Ballade III' by Christine de Pizan

I.

And as Leander crossed that salted strait,
alive at his skin to the water, in all its
unsettled electrolytes, all craftless and concealed,
a disappearing small packet of risk, breathing her name
into his fearful shoulder with every
fifth stroke, her home on the snatched in-breath.
As she waited, Hero, composed of that same, dark water:
look how love orders the lover.

Across the sound – from which
so many have shouted – our little Leander pants
for old love, unsatisfactory and noble, parcelled inside
the unfolded carnation of heat his chest holds
against the near-freezing water. Against that passage:
raw chance, the violence of numbers, voltage, charts
and patterns, the hubris of analysis, weather-fronts: a storm.
Foresight. See how love orders the lover.

Look how seeing preempts the gulf.
And Leander drowned himself in it, noble
and unsatisfactory. And Hero, in all things fit-for-purpose,
lost herself to it, too, at the same time as he,
if later. As this: one cause, one effect.
See this, poor etiolated lovers, at
the seafloor of love's furious cause:
look at how love orders the lover. Look

and learn nothing. I beg you.
This ordering, this deluging myth-kitty; we crave it
overrule our cretin solitude: are desperate for it.

Look at how love orders the lover.

II.

Always a line I told myself I'd never cross,
this retelling of the Greeks, a long game
I'm utterly without feeling for. And now (no hero, no claim
to heroism) I find you handing me the literal and I fold,
craftless and concealed in the face of
you, your mind, your body. Breathing the metre of it,
Medieval French to English. Parcelling something across.

Look how love orders the lover.

This sound, these English vowels I've made – if anything –
my home, I shout from them my hectors at the French.
Watch me struggle, craftless in the face of order.
Listen, Frenchy: the gap between our tongues
is just the blackest water, nothingy and unbreathable
with wordlessness, knowable at exactly and only those points at which
waves raise like scars from the skin
to catch that scattered, consonantal moonlight.

What survives the crossing? The correspondence
of two white corpses (*look how love...*)
pushed together by the tide of odds, these
devastated, idiolected lovers. Ten causes,
uncountable effects, a mess of want and
best guess, a sad seafloor of unthinkable love, everybody

just basically wanting to look good, everybody
just trying to write one good poem.
And to push it across, through the nasty insulation

of language, of the straight and the sound.
Don't stop. I'm sorry. Watch
for that washed-up body, white
and spoken with love.

A PICTURE

You'll have had me, the sight of me, down on the sand
in the wind, distant as the ships from the
shipping forecast we'll be ignoring
come quarter-to-one (being in bed, doing again

what we'd be doing next), caught on the empty strand
in the web of kitestring from the kite we'd won
on the arcades, its line as it flies dividing the beach, catching
the September evening's fibrous shine on its otherwise

vanishing fineness. You've a photo, in fact,
that's your battered laptop's desktop still.
Still, you won't have seen the three swans

painstakingly splitting the sky the sky
was determinedly becoming
as what happened next happened next.

FANTASY OF MANNERS

What is this Highway Code of need to behave myself, even
in the empty backroads of late at night? I feel to be
literally observing my own hailmary explanatory,

my pyrotechnic internal self-justificatory habitualism –
post hoc ergo propter hoc. Post hoc ergo bollocks hoc.
Bollocks hoc ergo proper shite. Shite bollocks ergo

propter shite and always allowing the bitter anaesthetic of intellect
to play across my hurts like sunlight
cancelling the water it returns from,

turning and re-turning in the retinal hollows,
cavernous and reptile. But no!, let us ply our tools,
though curious things they are,

delicate coils of meat and sugar
thriving in the marshy cloaca of the mind.
Let us bring our batteries to bear,

our coalitions of the will, and all the crashing
and imparallel highways of conjecture we have managed
to hold on to. Until

now. Until now. Until now, until now   set out
your little stall then, moment, lay the table
for a prissy meal of chitter, lamb and judge,

offer up the gentle pitfalls of conversation. Christ,
it's hardly *Gormenghast*.

A BRIEF GLOSA

I know that each one of us travels to love alone,
alone, to faith and to death.
I know. I've tried it. It doesn't help.
Let me come with you.
after Yannis Ritsos, Moonlight Sonata

Twenty-four days, really, all told,
straggling Manchester's dive-bars until five for the pretext of drink
between the kitsch and neons as if there was no agony
keeping our bodies apart. Three-something weeks there, and then
    perhaps
three-thousand emails, Manchester to France. Praise be for
    smartphones.
I know that each one of us travels to love alone,

but this – this is surely unnecessary. By the time you left we'd settled
to a nightly routine: The Temple, The Thirsty Scholar,
the failing Black Dog Ballroom, always open, desperately, until dawn
with always a floor to ourselves. The cluttered inbox of lust
already blinking in my chest. And then we left,
alone, to faith and to death.

As in the time you took me back to the place you shared
with your absent fiancé to read me the Greek
of Yannis Ritsos, in Greek, until the sounds
worked by your tongue brought your tongue too much
into focus. Certain lusts can be swallowed, that noble, necessary gulp.
I know. I've tried it. It doesn't help.

Ritsos, with his *faith* and his *death*, is thinking more
of that intricate momentary balancing act, the fiddle of drink and time
by which we can hope to produce our presentable selves;
the phone screens and mildewed old editions
of the old translations you left me, all we believed we could afford
to eschew. Let me come with you.

I AM POSITIONED

at the edge of whatever bridge this is called so the breakbeat/sitar
    fusion being
vaguely beatmatched by the dj on the bank below is ranged against
    the scope
of the busking clarinettist skipping through the klezmer songbook
    further down the bridge
and they both have those eerie semitone intervals so it's not

so discordant as it sounds. Also it's dusk so there's all this sunset in
    pastels chosen
by a tired and emotional aesthete coming up behind the huge lights
    on what must be
the Egyptian embassy and falling half on the embankment's
    concrete very smoothly
and half on the choppish Thames, where the pretence of surface

is shattered. But it's not about London's emulsion of cultures or
the fragmentary nature of modern life: it's about romance

because I'm thinking of the woman who has asked
for us to keep apart, for two months, while she

works things out: the woman I love. Although
I didn't, I suppose, make that clear.

    x   to mimic the slow pass
of memory, the glassy recollection of a cheap print
of a painting by Bonnard in the university bedroom
of an old friend. *x*   to pass the time:
to go past it, into the space of a page.
    x   as an excuse to sit, handled by the August sun
on a fourth-story Turinese balcony,
swallowed by the late afternoon heat
and Peter Sarstedt playing from inside,
moving your toes in a pool of shade cast
by the laundry drying on the storey above. *x*
to bring tokens of then and now into brief relation,
a lamp-shadowed, concentrating face into the
bright but declining North Italian sunlight.
    x   to prove something false about the endurance
of feeling the sun on one's face. *x*
like a gesture towards marble. Consider the way
uv-exposure lifts the tan to the surface of your skin,
as if risen from a health that rests in your
subdermal tissues, coddled around your bones. *x* to coax it. *x*
to winch the forms which once were ships of state
from out the greenish water, which won't
even for a moment quiet into the stillness
of a concentrating face, offset by the cheap print
on a Bonnard picture in your long-gone university
bedroom. *x* to retrieve the slow shelter of memory
and the love story below it,
all the bravura genitive syntax of desire
elected up from the tangled backstreets of memory,
flickeringly lamplit and persistent. *x*
because what else is there to do?
There is nothing: make friends with people

who will only subsequently insist upon
going on to die? Rescue from itself
a society which is constitutionally uninterested
in rescue, a princess in a tower with a jigsaw
of terrible beauty and seven billion pieces?
Cook and eat exotic dishes the subtleties of which
you cannot be equipped to taste? Haul up
the terrific wreck we've made of gender,
sunk into every one of our stories?
Haul that up, again? No,   *x*   in order
to linger on this balcony, hoping the striking
self-possession of the woman
smoking on the opposite balcony late last
night will reappear, her gathered-back ringlets:
her arms crossing and recrossing after raising her
cigarette to her lips, she reminded me of someone.

   x   because you have a strange internal grammar
which always uses the second person for self-reference
but also for the irregular but sudden and insistent
addressing of various archetypical
love interests.   *x*   to bring that idiolected grammar,
that ragged coalition of playing pieces from various
and even incompatible games, to bring it to the surface, like the tan
on the skin of the woman on the balcony on the courtyard,
across the courtyard, to whom you never will speak.

   x   in digression from your financial
and romantic perplexities.   *x*   because hope
is purer than happiness.   *x*   like you imagine
an existentialist might, bent over a coffee table
late at night, partially obscured
by an inherited piano, the lid closed and the key
lost long ago.   *x*   as if every moment's perception
was a new year's do and demanded a new
Auld Lang Syne all its own. A perception

of the host of miscellanea suspended above the street
by the opposite block's many balconies – potted azalea,
clayey spades, bales of cable, grey-mildewed notepads, a radio.

   x   in order to oblige a friend with whom
you frequently exchange work to visualise
a parade of new things – the apparently
random scatter of gothic chimneypots rising
asymmetrically from the terracotta of the opposite block's roof
or the naked body of a shared friend, the bold curves
of his calves, the sweep of his navel like an intake of breath
down towards the gentle axolotl of his penis.

   x   to insist it's okay that some things are
radically distinct. My love for you, for
each of you.   *x*   for that old story.   *x*   as if in song,
distracted by the song;   *x*
because what else is there to do? Watch *Amélie* again?
Mastubate in your flat's communal shower? Fantasise
about winning the lottery, of getting a flat
in the backstreets of Naples, with a balcony, watching the bats
flicker across the piazza flycatchers all, as if
from that confused movement you could take
what passes for an answer?

It's true the music here is plainsongy and austere
and there is little by way of gunpowder.
But I've learned that the fraction of what you will meet
in the world that is capable of requiting
anything is tiny and obscure. We make do. Frequently
I recount this self-destructive, back-biting anecdotal patter
amid the strange branches I've renamed myself. Make
do, and go out with a gag. God, for the tiny requital

of receipt, some relief across the home-made traps
and walls and hokey decoys. Which after all
are all the sign I have that something's out there.
I know that we have years – perhaps forever – to wait
until the drawling missionaries and the thrill and the skin drums
of pirates. And until then, I am bricking myself in.

ACKNOWLEDGEMENTS

I'd like to thank the editors of the publications in which some of these poems, often in earlier versions, first appeared: *PN Review*, *Poetry London*, *The Sunday Times*, *Best British Poetry 2014* (Salt), *Magma*, *The Rialto*, *Poetry Wales*, *The Lifeboat*, *Cadaverine*, *Best of Manchester Poets Volume 2* (Puppywolf), *Shearsman*, *Ambit*, *New Poetries VI* (Carcanet), *For the Very Last Time* (Ambergris Editions), *Poems in Which*, *Agenda*, *The Manchester Review*, *Stand*, *Laudanum Chapbook Anthology: Volume One* (Laudanum), *Lookout: Poetry from Aldeburgh Beach* (Lookout Editions), *The Tangerine* and *Blackbox Manifold*.

I'd like to acknowledge the previous translators of the reworkings in this book. These include (but are not limited to) Martin Sorrell, Richard Sieburth, Michael Hamburger, Jonathan Galassi, Jamie McKendrick, Edmund Keeley, Philip Sherrard, Maryann Corbett, Nancy Rose, Lyudmila Purgina and particularly Edwin Morgan.

Thanks are also due to the people who've helped me write this book: Nadia Connor, Chrissy Williams, Matthew Halliday, Stephen Nashef, James Horrocks, Aime Williams, John McAuliffe, Vona Groarke, Amy Key, John Clegg, Emily Hasler, Jon Sayers and Brenda Hillman. And especially, and enormously, to Jemima Foxtrot.